HEMINGF
is famo
enormous

To Mary

Mary Carter

14th November 1998

History Through Road Names

Mary Carter

Hemingford Grey is Famous for its Enormous Gooseberries -
History through Road Names

ISBN 0 9533940 0 X

Published by
Westmeare Publications
c/o The Norris Museum
St Ives
Huntingdon, Cambs PE17 4BX
UK

First published in 1998

Printed in England by
Victoire Press
1 Trafalgar Way
Bar Hill, Cambs CB3 8SQ

© Mary Carter 1998
All rights reserved

All profits will be donated to

The Friends of the Norris Museum and Library, St Ives, Cambs

Other Publications by the Author
"Town or Urban Society? St Ives in Huntingdonshire, 1630-1740" in Societies, Cultures and Kinship, 1580-1850, ed C Phythian-Adams
"The Hemingfords: A Local History Research Group", "Hemingford Abbots in the late 19th century; Some conclusions drawn from the census returns of 1851 and 1891" in Records of Huntingdonshire vol 3 No 5 1996
Not an Easy Church ... A History of the Free Church in St Ives, 1672-1981, (under the previous name of Mary Wagner)

INTRODUCTION

Hemingford Grey is famous for its Norman manor house, thatched cottages and distinctive church tower but few today would think of gooseberries. Yet the quotation, which forms the title of this book, gives us an endearing reminder of its past glories as seen by an older historian. Today farming is commercial and the Giddins gooseberry is only found in private gardens.[1]

Village histories can be written century by century, or under topics, such as farming, the manor, or new developments. We decided to use road names so that residents and visitors can see how they reflect our past. Some names are very old; for example, the Thorpe is a Danish word which reminds us of the earliest inhabitants. Other names recall the important buildings of the middle ages like Manor Road and Church Street. Mill Lane shows the importance of the river and watermills to the economy of the village. St Ives Road and London Road reveal the direction for travellers. The industrial expansion of St Ives led to the construction of Victoria Terrace in the reign of that Queen. Since the end of the Second World War the village has grown enormously and we pay tribute to the wisdom of those who chose names for the new roads that reflect people and places of the past.

Most of the book is written alphabetically under road names, but there is a brief history of the village at the beginning to set the background. There has been no attempt to write about all aspects of the past life of the village but only those that explain the choice of names. You can read the book from start to finish but the most important sections are Church Street, High Street and Manor Road.

Our group - Jan Biggs, Mary Carter, Peter Leary, Aileen Snudden, Rosemary Wright - derived indirectly from a WEA course on local history. This led to the setting up of the Hemingford Local History Society and an upsurge of interest in the history of the two villages. We have been assisted and encouraged by members of this Society, in particular Bridget Smith and Pamela Dearlove, and by many villagers. We would especially like to thank Bob Burn-Murdoch for the maps, and Stewart Denham for the cover, line drawings and invaluable advice on graphics. To everyone we wish to record our thanks in the hope that this method of linking road names to the past will give pleasure to the present.

(A map showing most road names in the village is on page 24)

HISTORY OF HEMINGFORD GREY

Although Celts, Romans, Saxons and Danes all lived beside the Ouse, they have left few records to help us understand the origins of the village. An intelligent guess suggests that the two Hemingfords once formed a Roman estate south of the important settlement of Godmanchester. With the departure of the Romans, the Saxons took over the land. In the ninth century they agreed to split the estate persuading the Danish invaders to settle in **the Thorpe**, Hemingford Grey, away from their own settlement in Hemingford Abbots.[2]

In the first record relating to the **manor** of East Hemingford (Grey) in 1041, not long before the **Norman** Conquest, King Hardecnut and his mother gave the manor to Ramsey Abbey "for the salvation of their souls and the soul of King Cnut".[3] This is the proper name of King Canute who is remembered for trying to stop the tide coming in, although it is more likely that he was trying to teach his courtiers a lesson that no king was all powerful and therefore he could not stop the tide. In 1066 the Abbot of Ramsey, the wealthiest landowner in this part of England, leased the manor to Aluric the sheriff who held the land by charter in return for military service. However, it was of little benefit to him as he was required to perform his military service shortly afterwards and died with King Harold at the battle of Hastings.

In 1086 William the Conqueror confirmed his gift of the manor to the Norman, Aubrey **de Vere**, who had been rewarded with the estates of Aluric the sheriff, chiefly in the counties of **Essex**, **Suffolk** and **Cambridgeshire**. In the Domesday Book Aubrey **de Vere** held the **manor** with two **mills** and a fishpool with 11 hides of land. A hide was a measurement of land, sufficient to support a family, and which a team of eight oxen could plough in a year.[4] It normally covered about 120 acres, suggesting that **de Vere** may have held 1320 acres.

His first known tenant was Ralf, son of Osmund, who was succeeded by his son **Payn** de Hemingford. He may have lived here as the **manor** house and parish **church** were probably built before his death in 1166. The house was protected by a moat which still exists on three sides. Possibly the modern river bed was the moat on the north side. The original river seems to be the backwater 100 yards further north. A ditch on the west side might be an outer or second moat. Equally it could have been a cutting to tie up a boat. There is an unproven theory that the Danes stored their boats here.

At this time there were probably 13 houses, with individual pieces of land attached, along the **High Street** and 8 along **the Thorpe**. The green lay between the **High Street** and the **Church**. Watermills which were an important part of the village economy had been in existence before the Domesday Book. The windmill was probably first built in the thirteenth century. The road through the village led from **St Ives** to Hemingford Abbots while an ancient track called the Mere Way, ran largely along the boundary between the two Hemingfords, across the A14, (the Roman Via Devana,) to Hilton. **Gore Tree Road** and **Long Lane** are other ancient roads.

After **Payn**'s death the **manor** was held by various members of the family including a granddaughter Alice who married Ralph de **Turberville**, hence the name Hemingford **Turberville**. A later descendant married John de **Grey**, from whom the modern name of the village is derived.

For four centuries the family owned the **manor** which was occupied by various relatives until it was inherited by George, the second Earl of Kent. In 1490 he had to surrender it to the Crown because of his debts. It was then leased to various nobles, including Edmund Dudley, Henry VII's favourite, and Richard Williams or Cromwell, great-grandfather of Oliver Cromwell.

The organisation of the **manor** affected the whole village. The manorial court was presided over by the lord or his steward with a jury composed of landowners or tenants to help decide cases. The court registered tenancies of land and settled disputes. For example, in October 1562, it was "ordered that no one shall glean in the fields before the rector has taken away his tithes, under pain of 3s 4d." In April 1626, Alicia Rignall, a widow, had still not repaired a dilapidated barn in spite of previous warnings, and at most meetings there were lists of people who had allowed their animals to graze on common land when this was forbidden.

The lord kept some land for himself, called the demesne, on which his tenants had to work. Probably this lay south of the **manor** house. In return villagers were given the right to grow crops in the open fields. They also had the right to graze animals. The **meadow**, whose bank protected the fields from flooding, was divided amongst the villagers and the lord of the manor. Grazing was allowed here once the hay had been removed. Gradually there was pressure to change the system. Tenants preferred to give their lord money instead of working on his land and wanted to convert tithes to money payments. Traditionally tithes were paid to the church in kind, that is a tenth of the wheat harvested etc. The change to payments of money reduced the opportunities for friction. There was also a movement to enclose parts of the fields instead of having strips scattered over the open fields with the court deciding on the crop.

The closing of the monasteries under Henry VIII in 1536 caused another upheaval. Whereas the rectory had belonged to the Priory of Huntingdon, it was now granted to a lay (non-Church) family, whilst the vicarage remained with the church. The rectory of Hemingford Grey, valued at £17 per annum, was leased firstly to Richard Wynde, a wealthy gentleman farmer from St Ives, then to William Muschamp and in 1600 to the Bishop of Ely. Owners of the rectory received the major tithes, that is a tenth of all the corn and hay grown, in addition to the profits from their own land. In 1636 the Bishop of Ely leased the site of the rectory, parsonage house, lands and tithes to William **Green**, a goldsmith of London who in turn leased them to Richard **Langley**. They were removed from the Bishop for a while during the Protectorate of Oliver Cromwell but returned when Charles II became King.

In 1574 the Crown leased the manor to Helen Marchioness of Northampton, who had invested in other manors locally. After her death it passed to two brothers called Ramsey. In the meantime money had been lent on the security of the lease by John Martin of Ely. A case was taken to the Court of Chancery, but before 1635 either by purchase or inheritance it passed to the **Newman** family, who seem to have been connected by marriage with the Martins.

There were a few early enclosures but more were made as a result of an agreement in 1628/9, repeated in 1670, between John **Newman**, the lord of the manor, his copyhold and freehold tenants of the manor and Richard **Langley**, the tenant of the parsonage. By this agreement some land in the common fields could be enclosed, provided tithes of grain and hay due to the Bishop or his tenant were converted to money payments.[5] The rate was ten pence per three acres enclosed and converted to pasture south of the Cambridge way where the land was heavy and further from the village or two shillings per four acres for land nearer the river. Tenants could only enclose 3 or 4 acres out of 20. As the document says, the enclosures were "for the gentle good and advantage of the whole town of Hemingford Grey." The document lists 65 landowners and tenants, out of a total population of just over 300. In 1674 a tax was levied on the number of hearths in a household. Of the 75 hearths in Hemingford Grey 53 were rated for tax and 22 exempted on the grounds of poverty, suggesting that at least 12 of the landowners were not resident as landowners would have paid tax.[6]

Enclosed land benefitted the farmer as he could convert arable to pasture. Cattle and sheep produced better returns than corn. By keeping his flock separate he also avoided the risk of infection from the village herd and could try to improve the quality of his animals by controlled breeding. But enclosure adversely affected others in the village who were left with a smaller common for their animals. Nor could they gain by grazing additional sheep and cows as that was strictly controlled. They were only allowed to pasture 3 milk cows, steers or young bullocks for each 20 acres they farmed, in addition to 15 sheep and 2 horses or oxen. "Ancient" cottagers were limited to 2 cows and 7 sheep and "new" cottagers to 1 cow and 1 young bullock.

To recompense the cottagers, an area called Breckney Marsh, divided from the Great Marsh by the lake, and land called Hassocks in Milne field could be used between St James' day (25th July) and May 1st. Cattle could also be staked on the balks which lay between the strips of crops until the common fields were open for grazing after the harvest had been gathered. The classical system of three field farming was in use. The Milne Field and Greenway Field were worked as one unit, Brookfield and Harland Field as the second and Thorpfield and Bushfield as the third. Two were cropped at a time and the third left "to lye fresh and fallow".

The Crown sold the **manor** again in 1704 to Cornelius Denne, a merchant of London. The surname Denne was common locally. Perhaps he was a relative now living in London. However, because of his debts it reverted once more to the Crown in 1711. In 1721 James **Mitchell**, another London merchant, bought the manor from the Crown. He was once described as a Scotch pedlar, "who travelled England with a pack upon his back and by the most unheard of Niggardliness and Parsimony became extremely rich and inherited large landed property in Huntingdon and Cambridge which included the Manor House at Hemingford Grey".[7] Today he would probably be admired for his initiative and enterprise. In 1703, he bought the Fowlmere estate in Cambridgeshire and in 1721 acquired Hemingford Grey and half of Hemingford Abbots.

By 1801 the population of the village was about 350 people. In that same year, the remaining 1110 acres of the manor were enclosed by Parliamentary decree.[8] To be passed the bill needed the support of three quarters of the landowners. The process allowed owners of land to exchange and consolidate their scattered strips in order to make manageable fields which could then be enclosed with fences and hedges. In general profits increased after enclosure. In Hemingford Grey, there were five large owners, the Bishop of Ely through his tenant had 358

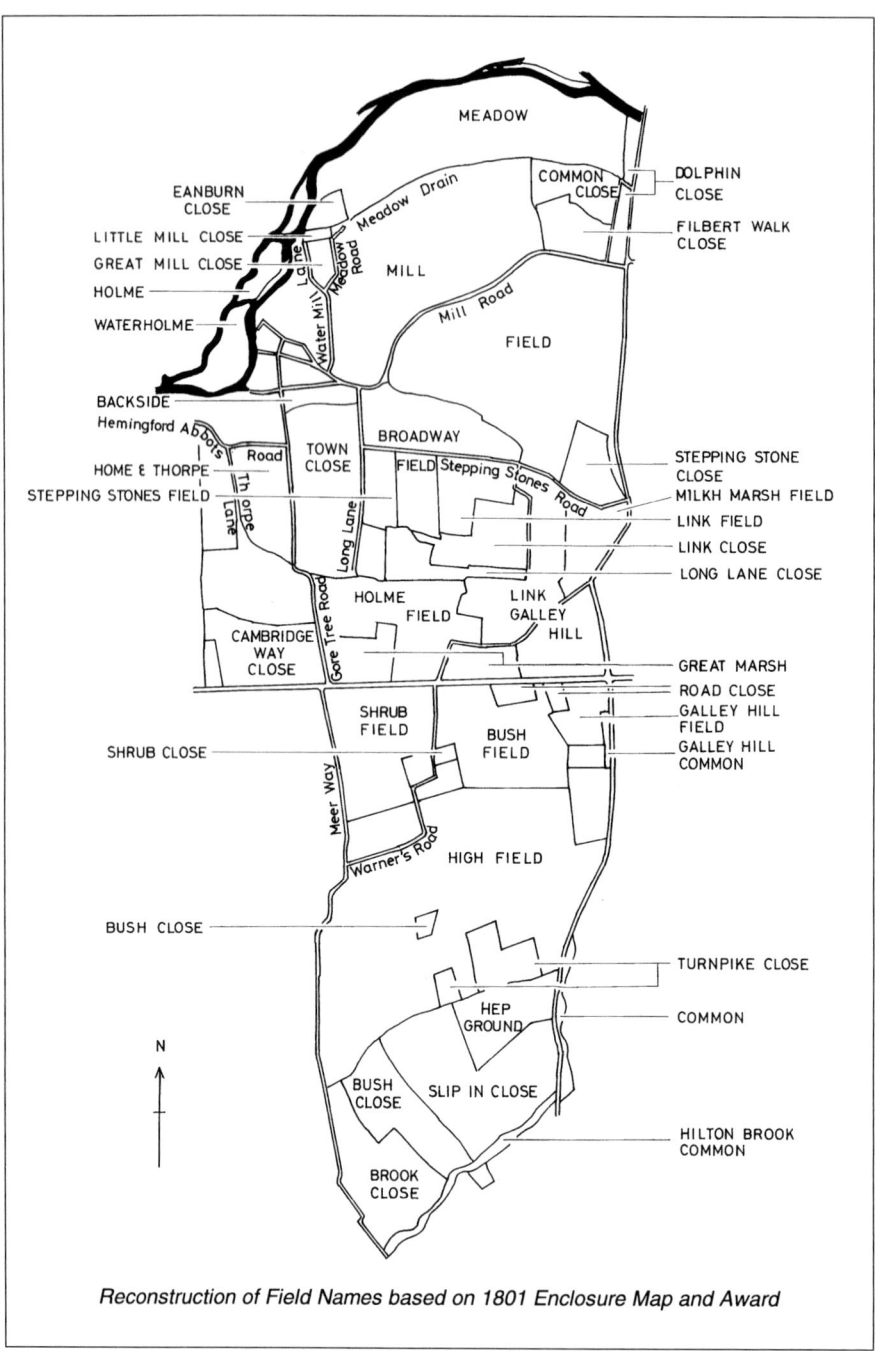

Reconstruction of Field Names based on 1801 Enclosure Map and Award

acres, the **Margett** family 174 acres, the **Mitchells** of the Manor House surprisingly had only 121 acres, J E Hovenden 119 and the vicar 74. This does not include the acreage previously enclosed.

The tenant of the bishop and vicar of Hemingford Abbots was Charles **Green**.[9] At the time of the Enclosure Award of 1801 his wife was known as the appropriator of the tithes as she was a layman. She was allocated 358 acres in compensation for surrendering the tithes which had formed so great a portion of her income. Monuments to her, her husband and various members of the **Green** family can still be seen inside the church.

As an effective working unit the **manor** ceased at this point. Some of its functions, dating back to the middle ages, were taken over by the vestry, including those of the meadow reeves and pinder. The former were appointed to look after the **meadow** and see that all the farmers kept to their strips, cut the hay on the correct dates and did not graze animals before the hay was harvested. To this day the village appoints two meadow reeves. The pinder looked after the **pound** where stray animals were held until claimed by their owners.

The population increased greatly in the nineteenth century from 350 in 1801 to 1258 in 1851. This was largely caused by three building developments, the workhouse in **London Road**, **Victoria Terrace** and the now demolished **Filbert's Walk**. This extension of the village shows the influence of **St Ives** as they were all within walking distance of the town with its greater opportunities for employment.

This was a period of great change in the village. Up until 1801 the houses were all contained within the area of the **High Street**, **Church Street** and **the Thorpe**. After enclosure, farms were built on the newly enclosed land and houses gradually spread beyond the core of the village. Public buildings were also erected. The church school was opened in the **High Street** in 1853 and a mission school was started in 1866 on **London Road** for the new inhabitants. The village workhouse in the **High Street** closed in 1836 and its inmates were transferred to the large Union Workhouse on **London Road** together with other poor people from the district. However, the workhouse cottages were still occupied by villagers. The nonconformist chapel was opened in 1853 and the reading room in 1898. In the middle of the century the railway was built across the meadow connecting St Ives with Godmanchester. It must have been a shock to the village when the vicar was killed by a train in 1899.

Further changes came with the agricultural depression of the late nineteenth century which severely affected farming in East Anglia. Imports of cheap grain from America and frozen meat from New Zealand and Australia almost destroyed many farmers with the result that the population decreased by 1891 to 883, and even reached 752 in 1921. People were forced or enticed to move away to employment in towns or even abroad. Administratively, there were great changes when the unelected vestry was superseded in 1896 by an elected parish council and all villagers were able to have some influence on decisions made.

Developments in the twentieth century have transformed the village. Its ancient heart is now surrounded by many new houses which have been built, not only individually, but as whole roads or estates. Few who live in the village were born there and fewer still are employed there. The population has increased enormously and continues to do so with the latest estate being developed off **Long Lane**. Although the village is now largely suburban, it has however remained an active community with a flourishing school, church, sports centre and host of different societies. It is very different from the early settlement on the Ouse whose inhabitants in times of trouble could take refuge in a fortified manor house.

ROADNAMES

APPLE ORCHARD   Although this name is not mentioned in the Enclosure Award of 1801, the lane existed in the nineteenth century when it led from Hemingford Road into an orchard which extended through to Marsh Lane. It was required for access to the newly enclosed fields.

BRAGGS LANE   In 1718 Mary Bragg, a widow, died. Under the terms of her will the vicar and churchwardens were to distribute "among the poor of that parish, having first regard to the poor old maids" one pound and ten shillings (£1.50p) in sums of one shilling and sixpence (7½p) and one shilling (5p) on St Thomas' Day, 21st December, each year. Five shillings (25p) was to be paid to the bellringers at the same time. The land she left was an "olyard in Mill Field in Olyard furlong and half an acre of meadow in the Great Meadow."[10] In the 1628/9 list of owners of lands and tenements in Hemingford Grey, Dorothy Bragg, a widow, is listed and in 1670 an Edward Bragg, presumably her son. Mary Bragg could conceivably be his widow.[11]

THE BRAMBLES   This road lies behind Limes Park. Waste water from the workhouse was pumped here. Later it was covered with brambles and was excellent for blackberrying.

BURLINGTON WAY   This was the first speculative building site in Huntingdonshire. It was started in 1957 by the developer Arthur Burling, hence the name. The "ton" was added as it was felt that it sounded better. When Mr Handley of the agents Witherow and Handley applied for planning permission he used houses from the game Monopoly to demonstrate the proposed layout. All sewerage was at first taken into pits in the front gardens until the arrival of main drainage. The selling price was £2200 with £230 for the extra room in the roof space.

CHURCH STREET AND CHURCH LANE (or Back Street)   The first church was probably built at the same time as the manor house by Payn of Hemingford who died in 1166. There may have been a central tower and north aisle, of which two bays remain. When the church was reconstructed in the 13th/14th centuries, it lost its central tower but acquired two longer aisles. The west tower was built in the 14th century and the clerestory in 1500.

At first, the church came under Huntingdon Priory, hence it was sometimes called Hemingford Priors to distinguish it from Hemingford Abbots, which belonged to the Abbot of Ramsey. It was founded as a rectory and the tithes

Church Street, once called Back Street, looking towards the river c 1930 (HRO PH43/80)

were paid to the Priory. When a resident priest was required, a vicarage was established and the tithes were divided; the great tithes of corn and hay being the property of the Priory and the small tithes of livestock, wool and non-cereal crops belonging to the vicar. After Henry VIII closed the monasteries in 1536 the rectory was granted to a lay (non-Church) family, whilst the vicarage remained with the church. One of the responsibilities of the rector, even if he was a layman, was to keep the chancel in repair and in 1859 the house belonging to the Rectory was sold to Mr John Lawrence in order to cover the cost of repairs to the chancel. The house is now known as the Hemingford Grey Study Centre and is used for conferences.

The terrible hurricane across the county in 1741 blew down several church spires, including that of Hemingford Grey. Instead of rebuilding the spire, the stump was levelled off and finished with the attractive stone balls set at the angles that can be seen today. Either it was too expensive to rebuild the spire or there was concern for the foundations of the church which are right beside the river Ouse.

Church and old Rectory, now Hemingford Grey Study Centre (M P Carter)

There are various stories about the church spire. The tradition that Oliver Cromwell, who lived in St Ives between 1631 and 1636, shot the spire off is attractive but untrue as the gale occurred one hundred years later. Another tradition says that the spire fell in the river making a hole and that the bells can be heard ringing in stormy weather. This cannot be true either as the present bells are dated 1724 and would have been in the surviving tower and not in the spire. It has also been discovered that the wind was blowing from the south west so that the spire could not be in the bottom of the river but is more likely to have fallen through the roof of the church.

An explanation was needed for the hole in the river, if it ever existed. Another tradition suggested that it was part of an underground tunnel used by monks from the manor house to go to the church. It is said that when the course of the river changed in the middle ages, it moved over the tunnel causing it to collapse. A Miss Herbert, who lived at the manor house in the 19th century, is said to have found the commencement of subterranean passages and with the consent of the landlord one was explored and was found to end under the site of some old cottages which had been pulled down. "She hoped to explore the other but was going away for the winter and owing to a change of plans gave up the tenancy of the house and so it was not explored but it is quite likely that this is the one which did lead to the church and I expect it would have been found full of water." Her old gardener said that his father had seen the tunnel which was wide enough for three men to stand in it side by side.[12] The present owners of the manor house have not found any tunnels.

DAINTREE WAY The Daintrees were a well-known farming family in the area. Richard Daintree farmed 620 acres in Hemingford Abbots in 1851, living for 22 years in the Manor Farm. His son Richard went to Cambridge University to study geology in 1852 but contracted TB. The best hope for a cure lay in sending him to a warm climate. He chose Melbourne where he arrived in time for the goldrush. He worked for the Government of Victoria's geologist a Mr Selwyn, who possibly was a relative of the Reverend Edward Selwyn, vicar of Hemingford Abbots. This would explain why the family chose Australia for his convalescence. Richard Daintree became famous for his geological surveys of North Queensland, finding both copper and gold. A river and range of hills are named after him. He returned to England in 1870 and became the Agent General for Queensland in London. However, the damp climate of England did not suit his health and he died in 1878 and was buried at Lolworth.[13]

DENDYS Walter Dendy Sadler was the son of a solicitor who exhibited at the Royal Academy for fifty years. He studied art in Dusseldorf, which he called "the finest art club in the world." Whilst there he realised that no English painter had attempted anecdotal painting. On his return to England, he began to paint dramatic pictures of "the good old times." He lived for 28 years at River House in Hemingford Grey and painted the Ouse many times. "Home, Sweet Home" was one of his pictures in which he used the inside of his own house as a setting with villagers as models.

DE VERE CLOSE After the battle of Hastings, William the Conqueror rewarded his Norman follower Aubrey de Vere, with the estates of Aluric the sheriff, chiefly in the counties of Essex, Suffolk and Cambridgeshire but including the manor of Emingeforde (Hemingford Grey) in Huntingdonshire. In 1155 another Aubrey de Vere was created Earl of Oxford and in 1194 Hereditary Great Chamberlain of England. He was the founder of the Hedingham Nunnery in Essex. The ancestral seat was at Castle Hedingham where the finest rectangular keep in England still testifies to the power of the family. The influence and wealth of the family lasted for five and a half centuries.

DOUGLAS CLOSE Henry James Sholto Douglas Esq (later Captain) of Claybrook Hall in Leicestershire married in 1846 Mary Mitchell who with her sister Anne inherited the manors of Hemingford Grey and Abbots from their father the Reverend James Dykes Molesworth Mitchell. There were twelve children from this marriage who reached the age of 21. Their son Lt Col Henry Mitchell Sholto Douglas inherited the estate after bequests had been made to his eleven brothers and sisters. He lived at Springfields in Hemingford Abbots until 1928/30.

FILBERTS WALK (or Greens or Green Walk) This was the name of a row of cottages which were pulled down in the 1960's. The earliest record is of a "waterbank formally called the sluce bank,"[14] part of the system for protecting the village from floods. There is still a footbridge over what was the sluice. In 1751 it was a footway "called Mill bank, otherwise Filby's walk". The name Filbert's Walk is possibly a corruption from this. Thomas Filby was a landowner in St Ives who ran the Crown Inn, the premier building in the town.[15] On the map of 1801, Filbert's Walk is the path which led through the fields from Hemingford Road to St Ives. In 1851 it is called Green or Green's Walk from John Green who built the houses in the 1820's, virtually as a suburb of St Ives. He had already built other densely packed houses for rent in the town.

Each small house had a low lying scullery, often flooded in winter, with a copper for heating water and space for coal. There was a kitchen/living room with three steps down to the front road, and above that one bedroom and a tiny landing room. Water had to be collected by bucket from one of the three pumps behind the houses. It was heated in the copper, then used in the tin bath before being

Filbert's Walk (S Denham)

thrown into the front ditch. There were often problems with sewage because of the frequency of floods and TB was common.

The census return of 1851 shows that the people living here must have been employed in St Ives. Seven were watermen working on the river, others were carpenters, cordwainers, tailors and shopkeepers. There was a boatbuilder, a fireman, a platelayer and a bullock shoer, none being born in Hemingford Grey. Ten came from St Ives but others from Bedford, London, Norfolk, Oxford, Ramsey and Wisbech. Of the 29 heads of household 15 were born near to Hemingford Grey and the rest from further afield.

By the time of the 1891 census, we can trace the decline of traffic on the river and the rise of the railway. Only one man worked as a waterman, but nine worked on the railway as labourers, platelayers, porter or signalman. Three were coal porters or carters. This trade would have grown with the use of the railway. The influence of St Ives was still very strong as even after 40 years only 5 of the heads of household were born in the parish of Hemingford Grey.

Number 31 Filbert's Walk illustrates the changes that were taking place in local industries.[16] It had belonged to John May who owned a fleet of river barges. But with the arrival of the railway this was a declining trade. He leased and then later sold the premises to John Harrison who needed space to expand his basket making business as well as barges to transport his willows and baskets. Although he only employed seven men the year round, he used seventy people as casual labour to cut and prepare the willows in open-sided warehouses to the rear of Filbert's Walk. Stripping willow was the first Spring job before gooseberry picking. At one time his firm was the largest willow growing business in England. Hundreds of baskets were required by farmers to get fruit or potatoes to market, the GPO used them to handle the mail, the Fire Service to filter water from ponds or rivers or the Royal Air Force for dirty linen. But after the Second World War the arrival of plastic containers and the import of cheap baskets from abroad led to the decline in the business which closed in the 1960's.

Filberts Walk was a sociable place with people sitting chatting on their front steps on summer evenings. In the middle of the terrace was a pub, The Green Man, with an archway giving access to the back road. The Harrisons lived in the bigger houses at either end of the row. But the frequent floods were bad for the health of the residents and in the 1960's all the houses were demolished.

GLEBE ROAD   The Glebe was land owned or leased by the vicar, which had probably been left to the church by parishioners. The land was in strips in the open fields or in the great meadow. This was one source of income for a vicar, the other being the small tithes from livestock, wool and non-cereal crops. To compensate for the loss of the glebe at enclosure, the vicar was given land between Gore Tree Road and Long Lane, the present position of Glebe Road.

GORE TREE ROAD   The word "Gore" means a triangular or irregularly shaped piece of land in the open. In 1801, Gore Tree Road was described as the public road that ran from the village and "continued southward in its ancient course to the Cambridge Turnpike Road which it enters nearly opposite Gore Tree." The road therefore pre-dates 1801. The farm on the A14 is called Gore Tree Farm.

GREEN CLOSE   Although there is an area of grass here, the name comes from an earlier owner of the land, Mrs Anne Green who was the appropriator of tithes at the time of the enclosure of the village. Further information about her family can be found under Church Street.

GROVE LANE   The name of a lane which runs south from the A14 to a farm of the same name.

GUNNINGS WAY   The most famous residents of the manor house were the Gunning sisters. William Mitchell, whose father had bought the manors of Hemingford Grey and Abbots, had married in 1731 a woman called Elizabeth Gunning, sister of John Gunning of Roscomon, Ireland. It was arranged that John Gunning and his wife would rent the Manor House. Here four daughters were born - Maria, Elizabeth, Catherine and Sophia, who died as an infant. The family gave up the tenancy before 1741.

Elizabeth Gunning

They returned to Ireland when John Gunning inherited his father's estates but soon ran into debt.[17] When Mrs Gunning realised the beauty of her two oldest daughters she determined that they would make great marriages in spite of their lack of wealth. The girls were presented at Dublin Castle. The story goes that they borrowed gowns from a theatrical wardrobe for the occasion. The Lord Lieutenant was so impressed by their beauty that he recommended to their mother that she should take them to London. Their debut in England was at the Huntingdon Assembly in 1750 where they aroused great curiosity and admiration. They moved to London and crowds followed them wherever they went. Newspapers reported their movements and copies of their portraits were sold by the thousand. On one occasion Lord Clermont and others drew their swords to allow the two girls to escape their massed admirers. On another occasion seven hundred people waited outside an inn all night to see Elizabeth enter her chaise en route to Scotland.

In spite of their poverty, Mrs Gunning achieved her aim as both girls married lords. The Duke of Hamilton was so overwhelmed when Elizabeth agreed to be his wife that he insisted on the ceremony taking place that night. The clergyman at first refused to perform this impromptu ceremony but the Duke insisted and was married at just after midnight to his beautiful nineteen year old bride with a curtain ring, as no other was available. Her sister Maria married Lord Coventry three weeks later. By the age of 25 Elizabeth had been widowed and remarried, this time to the Marquess of Lorne, later the Duke of Argyll. Maria died aged 27; the cause of death was thought to have been white lead used in a beauty preparation but was more likely to have been TB. Due to the skill of Mrs Gunning in arranging their marriages, the blessing of an Irish beggar used to be "May the luck of the Gunnings be upon you."

Because of the uproar at the way in which the Duke of Hamilton married Elizabeth Gunning, Lord Hardwick introduced into Parliament in 1754 a Marriage Act which was designed to end clandestine marriages. The Act declared that all weddings could only be solemnized after the publication of banns. No marriage could be performed except by a clergyman of the Church of England, although Jews and Quakers were excluded. It also provided that minors, like Elizabeth Gunning, must obtain the consent of parents or guardians. For the first time bound volumes of specially printed forms were to be used by vicars.[18]

HALEY CLOSE The houses on Haley Close were built by Ivor Stocker, a local builder and developer. The road was named after the new born daughter of Peter Dawson who was working with Mr Stocker. It is a rare example of the name of a road which does not have a connection with the history of the village.

HEMINGFORD ROAD (Mill Road or St Ives Road) On the 1801 map this road is called Hemingford Road or Mill Road. Today it is called Hemingford Road and St Ives Road. The latter name is obvious as the road leads in that direction.

The Windmill (S Denham)

However, it also emphasizes the importance of the market town. Other research that looked at the relationship of St Ives and villages like Hemingford Grey has shown that there was a close relationship between the town and its neighbouring villages and this appears to have continued.[19] For example, in the seventeenth century, some villagers chose to become members of the Baptist Church worshipping on the quay in St Ives as others now drive to its successor, the Free Church.[20] Victoria Terrace and Filbert's Walk were in practice designed as suburbs of the expanding town. Inhabitants of these cottages were generally not born in the village. But wealthier residents of the village had also moved there from St Ives, for example the auctioneer Alpress Ashton who lived in the Rectory in 1851. Twentieth century inhabitants, who visit the supermarket in St Ives, copy the journeys of our ancestors who walked or rode to the medieval fair or market.

The alternative name, Mill Road, derives from the windmill and should not be confused with Mill Lane which led to the watermill. A windmill probably existed from the thirteenth century, although the present structure dates from 1820. It stood outside the village on open ground to catch the maximum amount of breeze. It was operated in the nineteenth and twentieth centuries by the Watts family who had been millers in Huntingdonshire for generations, owning both post and tower mills. Their new mill was built on the mound of the post mill it replaced. The last of the millers in the family, Erastus Watts, was grinding corn on the day of his death, 23rd January 1933, in the last working mill in the county. Ken Ballard's book "Old Industries of St Ives" records that Watts' nephew, Joe Newell, spent many happy hours with his uncle and soon learnt that a well maintained mill needed only a fair wind to operate it correctly. Gales were always a problem, as without good braking, a mill could soon become a runaway. After Erastus' death, Joe and his aunt used to climb to the top of the mill with a wooden mallet to check that the braking chocks were in good and tight, a frightening experience in a gale, when one had to shout to be heard against the creaking and groaning of the timbers, the flapping of the sail boards and the motion of the cupola against the wind. Only the bottom two-thirds of the tower

The High Street c 1920 (HRO PH43/36)

remain today and it has been roofed over with a round cap.[21] The 1801 map shows the windmill isolated on the Hemingford Road, its neighbours being a cottage on the corner of Long Lane in one direction and the Dolphin Inn in the other. With the exception of the mills, all other buildings were grouped around Church Street, the High Street, and the Thorpe. This included the farmhouses. It is only after enclosure that farmers moved their houses and yards to their own land elsewhere in the village.

The village school on St Ives Road was opened in 1905 with the closure of the two earlier schools in the High Street and on London Road.

HIGH STREET The High Street has also been called Front Street to distinguish it from Back Street (Church Street), or Town Street and parts have been known as Waterside, Riverside or the Pavement.

It is possible that the land between the High Street and Church Street was once a triangular village green between the two important buildings, the manor house and the church. There were stocks, a pillory and a whipping-post at the point of the triangle by Apex House, (the old Waggon and Horses). This small area was called the village green and may have been the remnants of the larger area. The lane that runs from the High Street to Church Street has the unusual name of Cottmarole.

The High Street is the centre of the village. You can see this in the buildings; farmhouses, shops, comfortable eighteenth and nineteenth century homes, and pubs, some of whose trade would have come from the river. In Victorian times many of the significant buildings of the village were sited here on the north side of the road.

The Congregational Chapel opened in 1848. Mr Potto Brown, the wealthy miller from St Ives and Houghton and a great philanthropist, gave the site and the cost of the building, "a pretty village meeting house, in the simple Early English style."[22] The chapel was one of a group centred on Houghton whose leader was Potto Brown. Even in his seventies he would walk from Houghton to Hemingford for a prayer meeting and he described in a letter to a friend how he had to rest on a gate to recover his breath and strength to enable him to continue his walk home. In time the number of members decreased and those who remained did not have the finances to keep the building in good repair. After standing empty for some years it was sold and converted into a private house.

The school, which opened in 1853 on land given by Mrs Desborough, cost £387. It may have replaced an older school. It was a National School (supported by the Church of England but with Government grants) and earned its income from "subscriptions and children's pence."[23] In 1851 the "school keepers" were aged 65 and 62 for roughly 100 children. The average attendance of about 40 shows that many only went if if they were not working and their parents could afford it. By 1891 education was compulsory and more organised. The schoolmaster was aged 27 and he had a pupil teacher, aged 15, and a monitor, aged 14, as helpers. The school closed in 1905 and was converted into the Church Rooms.

The Reading Room, built to commemorate Queen Victoria's Jubilee, was planned in 1897, although the foundation stone was not laid until 1898. The money was raised by public subscription. The land had been the site of the former workhouse, opened in 1778. Potto Brown had paid for the cost of the Congregational Chapel and it was his son Bateman who provided some of the 300 books for the Library which were a source of great pride. Bateman Brown was living at the time in Hemingford Park, in Hemingford Abbots. Villagers could sit around the fire reading the daily papers or playing games such as billiards and whist. The magnificent cup for billiard matches is now awarded for the winning organisation in the annual quiz. The Reading Room fell out of use in the 60's and 70's but was revived by amalgamating the Workhouse and Langley Charities, which then sold the only remaining workhouse cottage and used some

The Reading Room and Church Rooms, previously the Village School (P Leary)

of the proceeds towards repairs which were much needed. The Reading Room was re-opened in July 1984 and is used as a village hall.

The 1851 census gives us an idea of the people who lived and worked in the High Street. These included the Hardys who lived from the rents of property they owned and from annuities, Samuel who ran the Six Bells, Benjamin Gifford, the miller, who employed 12 men, Alfred Newton, a solicitor, the vicar and three single ladies, the Misses Ellen, Sophia and Liddia Margetts with their two resident servants. Other members of their family had owned the two houses on the corner of Braggs Lane, now called Broom Lodge and Harcourt. The publican at the Cock, now the only remaining pub, also worked as a farrier. There was another group of tradesmen that included a butcher, pig jobber and seller, cordwainer (leather and shoe worker), coal merchant, tailor, millwright, postmaster, waggoner, blacksmith and, surprisingly, a violin player. One wonders what kind of living he made. As his wife and son were both described as agricultural labourers, one assumes his earnings from music had to be supplemented. However, it can be seen that the villagers could buy most of what they needed for every day life in the village, but would go to St Ives for the market and for more unusual purchases.

There was a William Woods, a coachbuilder's man. In 1854 he recorded his thanks to "the Gentry and the Public of the county, for the extensive patronage they have enjoyed for so many years at Hemmingford, and beg respectfully to state, that they have erected and opened extensive premises near the station at

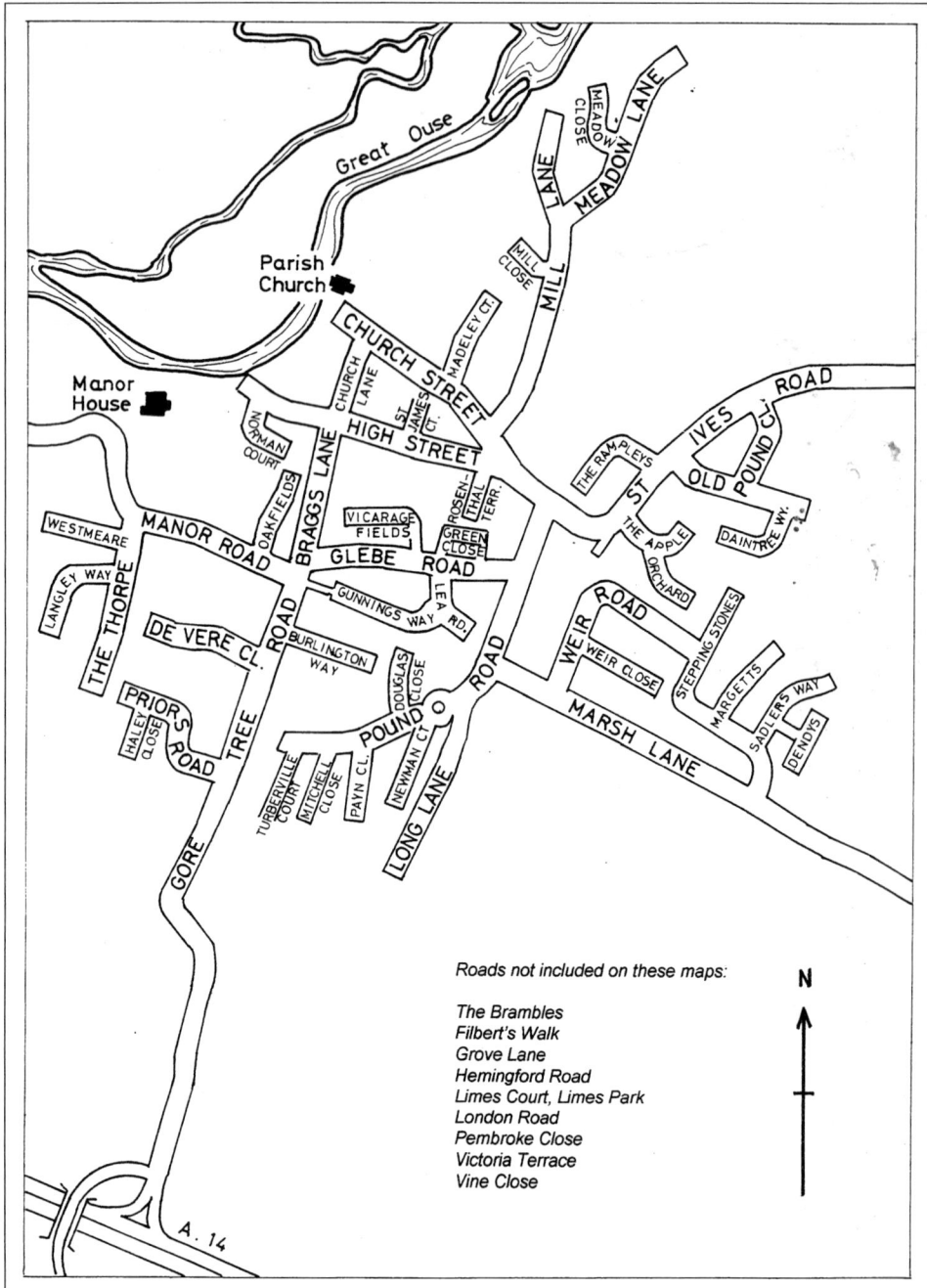

Map of the centre of the village with a

otograph taken in the 1970's

The High Street (P Leary)

St Ives, where they solicit an inspection of their stock of carriages, gigs, & of every description." The business flourished, even exporting the Ivo Cart to the United States. It eventually closed in 1894 and Woods returned to Hemingford to continue working as a wheelwright.[24]

Some who lived in the High Street worked on the land. They were mostly agricultural labourers but included others who worked in the market gardens and orchards. A widow, Mary Watts, was a cow keeper, whose daughter Ester seems to have run the household as there were six other brothers and sisters who had jobs as well as two children at school. Another widow, Lucy Favel, described herself as a charwoman. She had two sons working on the land, a daughter described as a servant, four children at school and a two year old at home. Various people were supported by the parish, the oldest being Catherine Setchell at 89 and John King at 85.

The 1891 census shows the changes in the economy of the village. There was still a shoemaker, wheelwright, miller, maltster, carpenter, baker and coal hawker. Others were still working on the land. Miss Lydia Margetts was still there with her widowed sister and two servants. But new industries had brought new occupations. Samuel Page worked on the railway, Charles Macrow was a French polisher, James Toller a florist. David Sneesby drove a ginger beer van, perhaps for Wadsworths in St Ives. Frances Darlow was a telegraph clerk. A banker, Mr Bevan, in what is now St Francis House, supported a wife and four

Messrs Giddings' boathouse and parish Church c 1920 (Norris Museum HEM.G/40)

children with the assistance of a cook, nurse, parlourmaid, nurserymaid and coachman who doubled as gardener.

In the early years of the twentieth century, visitors could hire boats at the end of the High Street from Mr Giddins. Afterwards they could enjoy something to eat or drink in the Tea Rooms or watch from the balcony. One of his advertisements describes his main business as follows; "Messrs Giddins & Son undertake River Boat Building in all its branches, and are Contractors for Boathouses, Wet Docks, or Houseboats, for the Repair and Renovation of Boats and for the Housing and Storing of Boats by the season etc."

LANGLEY WAY There were two Langleys connected with the village. Richard Langley lived at the rectory at the time of the Civil War. The house and lands were leased by the Bishop of Ely to William Greene and he in turn leased them to Langley. There was an agreement in 1628/9 that land in the open fields could be enclosed, provided tithes of corn were converted to money payments. The money was his recompense for not receiving his portion of the crops.

Local tradition has it that in the Civil War Hemingford Abbots supported the King and Hemingford Grey the Parliament. In 1642 the King, needing funds to begin the war, persuaded the colleges of Cambridge University to give up their silver plate. Parliament tried to intercept the wagons at Lolworth thicket. Under the guidance of the vicar of Great Gransden, the first portion avoided the Parliamentary army to reach the King at Nottingham. Subsequently two men were fined by Parliament, one of whom was Richard Langley, now an old man of seventy. He pleaded that he was only a spectator with hundreds more when the University plate was taken through the county. He had never acted against Parliament. He had paid his taxes, and sent a dragoon, horse and arms, presumably to join the Parliamentary army. His fine of £75 was reduced to £50 because of his pleading. The second man was fined £233, because he accompanied the silver to the county border.[25]

His son, Robert Langley, is better known. By his will of 1656 he left land in the Isle of Ely, the rent of which was to be distributed "to poor widows and others of the poorest sort" and to pay bellringers. The money was said to be used to commemorate the time when he was lost in snow in Hemingford meadow, whilst walking from St Ives to Godmanchester. Hearing the bells of the Parish Church he discovered where he was, and said that ever after the bells should ring each year on the same date to commemorate his escape. It is a delightful story which has been recorded for at least three other parishes in Huntingdonshire. Unfortunately, it is not true as his will said that the money was left in memory of his father.[26] The money from his charity, combined with the workhouse charity, was used to repair the Reading Room and is still used to help villagers who are in need.

LEA ROAD A lea is usually arable land which has been temporarily laid down to grass.

LIMES PARK AND COURT This is the site of the St Ives and Union Workhouse which was constructed in 1836 to house the people on relief in 21 local parishes. Each parish had to provide its share towards the total cost of £4000. Spaces were provided for 400 inmates, although in 1871 the total present for the census was 124, 72 males and 52 females. Men and women lived in separate wards radiating from the governor's house in the middle. Census returns show that very few were born in Hemingford Grey. Everyone was expected to work for 10 hours a day, often untwisting old ropes to make oakum, used in caulking the seams of ships.

In time workhouses developed into orphanages and sometimes hospitals for the "feeble-minded", the aged and the infirm. Although all parish relief was meant to

Limes Park, once the St Ives and Union Workhouse (P Leary)

be distributed through the workhouse, we know that people were able to remain in their homes in the village rather than suffer what was seen as the indignity of being sent to the workhouse. There were occasions, however, when a woman would be admitted for the birth of her child and then returned home afterwards. It closed in the 1930's and was converted into housing, then refurbished in more recent times.

Limes Court extends behind the garage.

LONDON ROAD   This road has been called Potton Way, Potton Turnpike Road, Ware Road, Union and London Road. It lies along the boundary between the parishes of Hemingford Grey and Fenstanton. Roads that form a boundary are often extremely old.

The road led to a ford over the river Ouse now crossed by the fifteenth century bridge. It was the land route to the famous medieval fair of St Ives and there was a causeway here from a very early date. For their use of the causeway, the abbots of Ramsey had to pay each year to the lord of the manor, one pair of scarlet hose, 2 lb of pepper, 2 lb of ginger, 1,000 eels and the right to cut wood. The rent was altered in 1238 to 40 cartloads of wood, 1,000 eels and half a mark. John de Grey agreed to a cash sum of 2 marks and a promise to maintain the causeway. Because of problems over maintenance this charge was converted in 1625 to an annual payment of 26s 8d. In 1822 the Duke of Manchester who owned the manor of St Ives, replaced the ancient causeway called Helford Bridge with the "new bridges". It has also been known as Coles Hill after a tailor, Mr Coles, who lived in Bridge Terrace.

The Dolphin Inn lies at the foot of the bridge and has been an inn for many centuries. Edmund Pettis records in his Survey of St Ives that in 1616 the fairs and markets of St Ives were leased out together with a messuage called the Dolphin and four acres. Sometime later the Dolphin Close, holts, and fishing were "sold from the baileywick".[27] Prior to this sale the Dolphin must therefore have come under the jurisdiction of the bailiff of St Ives. At the time of the enclosure award in 1801 the inn was owned by John Hodson, in 1851 by Sarah Reve from St Neots and by 1891 by Albert Edward Worts from Waterbeach, described as a castrator and innkeeper. Bridge House, a merchant's house and yard next door, on the other hand was the home of the Lindsell family for the whole of this period.

With the exception of the Dolphin and the house next to it, there were no buildings in the parish on London Road until after the enclosure award of 1801. Then came Victoria Terrace and Filbert's Walk. This led to a demand for a school and by 1861 one was built near the workhouse. The schoolmistress in 1885 was called Florence Nightingale! The school could accommodate 100 pupils but had an average attendance of 61. It closed its doors in 1905 when the school on St Ives Road opened and is now a private house.

In 1836 the St Ives and Union Workhouse was constructed. This is now Limes Court and Park and has been described under these headings. Several other large houses were built in the nineteenth century. What is now called Armes Corner is named after publicans of the New Crown Inn which closed in 1967.

LONG LANE This is one of the old road names in the village. In 1801 it was a private lane running from Mill Road south. The only building was on the corner, although the first workhouse had been originally built opposite the junction. Long Lane farm was not built until after the enclosure of the open fields.

MADELEY COURT In 1801 a landowner called John Ekyn Hovenden and his wife Catherine lived in a big house on the site of Madeley Court. Between them they owned at least 120 acres in the village, to the value of £158 per annum. This made them the fourth biggest landowner. Subsequently General and Mrs Brooke lived in the house. The Hunts Post reported in 1904 that they had returned to the house after an absence of six months whilst alterations were made. "Another storey has been added and the architect is to be congratulated for the skillful and artistic way in which he had the improvements carried out by

New Crown Inn on the corner of London and Hemingford Rd c 1908 (Norris HEM.G/10)

Mr Skeels of St Ives."[28] Later Reid Adams who was the first mayor of St Ives lived there. In the Second World War St Augustine's Abbey school from Ramsgate was evacuated to the building. When the school eventually moved out, the house was demolished to make way for modern homes.

MANOR ROAD Manor Road only acquired its name in 1938; before that it was called Hemingford Abbots road.

The name recalls the early history of the village. Aubrey de Vere was given the manor of Hemingford Grey as a reward for his part in the invasion and conquest of England by William the Conqueror. His first known tenant was Ralf, son of Osmund, who was succeeded by his son, called Payn de Hemingford. Payn may have lived on the manor as the main block of the present manor house was probably built before his death in 1166, at the same time as the parish church. The house was originally conceived as a two storey building with storage space on the ground floor and a hall upstairs, open to the rafters, which was approached from the south by an external staircase or ladder. A fireplace was built for the upstairs hall. Norman windows can still be seen on the south, east and west walls. The house was protected by a moat which still exists on three sides of the house.

After his death the manor was held by various members of the family including a great-granddaughter Alice who married Ralph de Turberville, at which period the manor was called Hemingford Turberville. A later descendant married John de Grey, from whom the modern name of the village is derived.

Documents show that the Grey family were lords of the manor between 1256 and 1490. Possibly John de Grey lived in the house for some of the time as he transacted business here in person. In 1321 his son is described as having a chapel and chaplain in the house.[29] The chaplain was to celebrate divine service daily in his chapel "for the souls of Matilda de Grey his mother and all the faithful departed". It is possible that the foundations of the chapel are to the east of the Norman house, under buildings which are thought to have been first built in the fourteenth century. He used land in Papworth St Agnes to provide money to the prior and convent of St Mary's in Huntingdon to support the chaplain. This could account for the tradition that the house once belonged to monks. The manor descended through various relatives until it was inherited by George, the second Earl of Kent in 1490 who forfeited it to the Crown because of his debts.

Around the sixteenth century improvements were made to the house. A great central chimney was built in the lower part. This allowed the ground floor to be divided into two rooms heated by the new fireplace. At least two rooms were also formed on the first floor and a staircase inserted. Possibly at the same time two other rooms were made under the roof.

Between 1574 and 1721 the manor belonged to various people including the Marchioness of Northampton. Before 1635 either by purchase or inheritance it passed to the Newman family. Scratched to one side of a window in the music room of the house are two letters T/E N 1689. This could refer to Thomas or Elizabeth Newman. The manor was sold again in 1704 to Cornelius Denne, a merchant of London, and later to James Mitchell, another merchant from London. He also bought half of the manor of Hemingford Abbots.

His son William lived occasionally in the house and it is probably now that it was extended to make it into a Georgian mansion with a fashionable brick frontage to the river. The north wall was replaced with a brick facade with sash windows on three floors. At the same time the line of the building was extended to the west with possibly five windows on each floor. You can still see where the windows have been moved in subsequent alterations although the extension to the west

South Facade of the Manor House (by kind permission of Mrs D Boston)

has disappeared. There may have been a fire which caused so much damage that the whole extension was pulled down.

The most famous residents of the manor house were undoubtedly the Gunning sisters. They took London society by storm in the 1740's becoming the most admired women of their day. Although they had no rank or wealth their mother was determined to capitalise on their beauty and dangled for suitors of the highest rank. In this she was successful as both girls married lords.

Their uncle, William Mitchell, was possibly glad to have a relative in the house as it reinforced his links with the area which were not good as he largely lived in Surrey. The property passed to Knight George Coote Mitchell in 1798 who was named lord of the manor in 1801 but died intestate in 1814. His brother, the Reverend James Dykes Molesworth Mitchell, rector of Gunton in Northamptonshire, inherited the manor. Two daughters, Mary and Anne, were born in 1821 and 1824. The Reverend James died in 1838 leaving the two girls as heiresses. In 1846 Mary Mitchell married Henry James Sholto Douglas Esq, (later Captain) of Claybrook Hall, Leicestershire, and by this marriage obtained ownership of the manors of Hemingford Grey and Abbots. Her sister, Anne, never married. She was described in 1862 as being of unsound mind and the estate was administered on her behalf. Anne died in 1891 in the Isle of Wight, Captain Sholto Douglas in 1892 and Mary, his wife, in 1897.

The Mitchells rented out the land and house. In the early years of the nineteenth century a Mr Smith farmed the land. Between 1851 and 1861 the house was occupied by his widow Elizabeth, who was farming 200 acres with the help of eight men. Her brother was William Margetts, from an important village family. Then Mrs Herbert, a relative of the Rector of Hemingford Abbots, and her daughters lived in the house for many years, followed by an auctioneer from St Ives and then the grandmother of Michael Heseltine, the Conservative politician. Lt Col Henry Mitchell Sholto Douglas preferred to live at Springfields in Hemingford Abbots. In 1928/30 the estate was broken up and sold. The house was advertised for sale for £1,200 with three and a half acres of land.[30]

Joseph McLeod, who later became a BBC producer, lived in it before the famous children's author, Lucy Boston, bought the house in 1938. She used her imagination and the house which she loved so fiercely, to weave stories like "The House of Green Knowe," much loved by generations of children and since televised, inspiring a huge number of followers especially in Japan. Mrs Boston restored the house to its present state and also designed the lovely gardens. She spent the winter embroidering patch work quilts or writing and the summer working in the garden.[31]

She was a determined woman. Her house was called the Poltergeist House by local boys who would run past it without stopping. She and her son had some spooky experiences at first, with banging on doors which when opened revealed no-one and feelings of some malignant force. During the war she and her friend the artist, Elizabeth Vellacott, entertained air crew from RAF Wyton to musical evenings as their contribution to the war effort. But there were suspicions that Lucy Boston was a spy and her activities were investigated although they were never stopped. Today the house is open to the public so that people can see the mementos from her books, the beautiful quilts, the music room used in the war and the lovely gardens.

MARSH LANE The alternative name in 1801 was Stepping Stones Road and there are still people who can remember the stepping stones which crossed the stream.

There were two areas of marsh, one at the end of Marsh Lane where it joins London Road on the south side, which was called "Milkh Marsh", - presumably cows were pastured here. On the opposite side of the Lane was Stepping Stone Close. The Great Marsh was the land along the Cambridge Road on its north side. This was divided into small fields of about two acres each at the time of enclosure.

MEADOW CLOSE AND LANE Just beyond Meadow Close, Meadow Lane crosses the remains of the old meadow bank where boards used to be placed in times of flood to protect the village. At the old railway crossing the right of way then enters the Great Meadow (50 hectares) and crosses to the Dolphin Hotel, providing the shortest route from the village centre to St Ives. The meadow is separated from what was the open Mill Field to the south by a ditch and bank which was probably built in the 13th century to protect the crops. Up until 1910 the meadow was still divided into 29 strips (24 owners) marked only by wooden stakes. By 1997 the number of owners was reduced to five. Due to its botanical and historic interest, the meadow is now part of the Countryside Stewardship Scheme which pays the owners to protect the flora, continue traditional management and increase public access.

Flood meadows are invaluable because they are fertilised by silt deposited by the river. For many centuries, meadow land was far more expensive than agricultural land. Not only did it provide grazing but the hay crop was the "fuel" for transport and enabled animals to survive the winter. Until enclosure, landowners had the right to graze their animals after the hay crop had been removed. At enclosure, farmers were allocated a share of the meadow in addition to arable land but cottagers lost grazing rights.

As the path to the meadow crosses the bank there is a close on the left hand called Eanburn, Oubourn or Wobourn Close. In the fourteenth century the Abbot of Wobourn held in the village one messuage (house) and 60 acres of land, valued at a shilling a year. Possibly the name records this ownership. If so, it is ironic that it seems to have been a dissenting burial place in the 17th and early 18th century. Written in the parish register is "Amongst the burials are several entries of Burials having taken place at Oubourn or Wobourn in this parish, there are 17 such entries, the earliest being in 1687 and the latest in 1721, some of them were from neighbouring parishes. No doubt this was a dissenting burial place; but so far local enquiries have failed to elicit any information about it." At that time, any burial in the churchyard took place according to the rites of the Church of England even if the family had worshipped in a chapel or Quaker meeting house. Therefore, some dissenters chose to use other burial grounds where the service could be conducted by a minister of their choice.

MILL LANE AND MILL CLOSE The Domesday Book of 1086 recorded that there were two mills and a fish pool which provided a total profit of £12 to Aubrey de Vere, the lord of the manor. By 1279, Reginald de Grey was accused of diverting the course of the river by making a pool between Hemingford and Huntingdon. He needed the mill pond and dam to increase the flow of water to his mill for grinding corn, but at the same time he made it difficult for ships and boats to travel to Huntingdon. What is now a backwater to the north of the main channel may be the original course of the river. In 1376 the same type of obstruction led to another petition to Parliament. At this time, the river Ouse was a major transport route for merchants who came from the continent to the great fair of St Ives. Even the king sent his stewards to buy cloth for the royal household. But as the population of the country increased, more grain was needed, demanding more mills. Mill ponds and dams were convenient for millers but made transport difficult for watermen. By 1534 we are told that there were four watermills in Hemingford.

At the beginning of the seventeenth century there was national concern about the state of the river. A report to the Privy Council in 1618/19 reported that the Ouse "that goodly fair river" was "generally foul and overgrown with weeds" and "stopped with weirs" between Huntingdon and Ely. The report suggested that the river should be cleared so that a better flow of water would prevent the disastrous floods which were so common in the area. Because of obstructions, merchants taking goods from Kings Lynn to Bedford, unloaded them at St Ives for onward transport by road. However, road transport was extremely slow and all heavy goods were wherever possible sent by water. It was the coal merchants of Bedford who took the lead in improving the flow of the river. By 1625 they

The Watermill and the Huntingdon to St Ives railway line (Norris Museum HEM.G/64a)

ensured that the river was made navigable as far as St Neots and by 1638 Great Barford. However, work ceased during the civil war.[32]

There was another petition of complaint in 1669 that "since the sluices (locks) were erected, all the rivers are so shallow and grown up, that where the said great barges did usually pass with from 26-30 chaldrons of freight, now flat bottom'd lighters with 8-10 chaldrons of coal cannot pass without great difficulty and charge and delay for want of water." A chaldron was 36 heaped bushels. Things once more improved in 1674 when Henry Ashley acquired the navigation rights and cleared the river again to Great Barford and by 1689 to Bedford. Staunches were built to provide relatively deep water for the boats. Conflicts continued between the demands of the millers, the watermen and the farmers who wanted good drainage for their land. It was not until after the Second World War that one body was set up to deal with these conflicting needs.

The toll book for Hemingford Sluice has survived for part of 1710.[33] It records that the following loads were taken upriver; wheat, barley, fish and freestone to Bedford, pots to Tempsford, fish to Wyboston, oats to St Neots, turves to Eaton, and more pots to Godmanchester. Goods going down stream were malt and wood. Although the names of 50 people were recorded, none were from the village, most of them being from St Ives, Huntingdon and Bedford. The advantage to the local economy would have lain in feeding the watermen and their horses, although this must have been balanced by the harm done by the horses if they strayed into the hay fields along the river bank. Until the arrival of the railway in 1847 the river continued to be the main transport route for heavy goods. By the beginning of the twentieth century, the railway was dominant to be superseded in its turn by road transport when Dr Beeching closed the railway line in 1959.

Between 1851 and 1891 Thomas Knights and his family worked the surviving watermill, with the help of nine men and two boys. They were a wealthy family. One son became an accountant, another a pharmacist and the remaining seven children were taught at home by a governess. Mrs Knights was assisted by two resident maids. The family also operated the steam mill of Alpress Ashton in the Low Road, Fenstanton. But fierce competition came in the form of the new steam mill built by Henry Goodman and Potto Brown at St Ives. This mill was built to the latest French design whereby the corn was emptied into a deep chamber at the top of the mill and not touched by hand until it was sacked up as flour at the bottom. Goodman and Brown were farsighted enough to see the importance of transport, because access to their mill was by river, rail or road. The Knights family, milling the traditional way by water power down a side lane in the village, were not in a position to offer vigorous competition. Today the mill has gone, and only the mill house, rebuilt in 1800, remains.

Fishing then as now was a popular pastime and fishermen's stories can be found in the local papers. There are a series of reports of sturgeon of great size being seen in Six Gate Pit. In 1903, 300-400 people gathered to watch Harry Thornhill, the bailiff of the Ouse & Nene Fishery Board, land a sturgeon. In 1907 the crowd was said to be between 1500 and 3000 as it was a Bank Holiday. The plan was to catch the giant fish cut it into steaks and sell it to raise funds for the County Hospital. In spite of many helpers, including well-known village folk, Giddins, Woods, Giffords and Dendy Sadler, only two fish were caught and neither was a sturgeon. When a roach was finally caught a wag called out "Get a worm!" Others suggested "that the fish existed only in the disordered imagination of certain fishermen whose long and unrewarded vigils had turned their brains." In 1924 there was another attempt led by Mr Knights, the miller, and a sturgeon

Goodman and Brown's steam mill, St Ives, with the causeway and railway (HRO WH2/12)

eight feet long was caught weighing 185 pounds. The fish was accepted by the Lord of the Manor, Colonel Douglas.[34]

There was excitement in 1919 when German prisoners were helping to clear the river. They brought up some brass vessels which were thought to have been dropped by monks when they fled from the manor house at the time of the dissolution of the monasteries.[35] Edward Linton Watts of St Ives was asked to investigate and he wrote: "Edward Holley who is ganger for the German prisoners working on the river was at Huntingdon. He has the vessels. At present I do not feel inclined to approach him but am trying to get the information you desire. I am rather sceptical about them ...Holley is sure to be on the make if possible and I think may be suspicious of any enquiries. Dendy Sadler is believed to have written the particulars for the 'Post'. He is rather opinionated. I do not know him nor wish to approach him." (Dendy Sadler was a famous artist who lived in Riverview House.) A second letter confirms his first opinions. "I have seen the vases. I am afraid they are a dud. They are probably not more than fifty years old. The style of the figures may be Georgian but the composition is probably inferior. I expect they were thrown away as worthless."

It is interesting to see that the tradition about the monks has continued from generation to generation although there is little basis for it.

MITCHELL CLOSE   In 1721 James Mitchell, a merchant from London, bought the manor of Hemingford Grey from the Crown. Further details about this family can be found under Manor Road.

NEWMAN COURT   John Newman acquired the manor of Hemingford Grey and part of Hemingford Abbots sometime before 1628/9. He seems to have been a resident. He and his grandson Mark were lords of the manor in 1628 and 1670. In fact, John figures in national records in 1630 as having "enclosed 106 acres of arable land lying in the common fields."[36]   In 1649 Richard Newman of Hemingford Abbots was fined for assisting the King in the Civil War. In 1680 Thomas Newman left the sum of £171 in his will, which was made up of the tithes owing to him, some cows, sheep, wool and hay. Assuming he was the current lord of the manor this was not a great sum. The properties in the two villages seem to have been shared amongst different members of the family. In 1698 Mark and his wife Elizabeth, Richard Newman and two others conveyed the manor to Thomas Newman, who died in 1715, at the great age of 90 and is buried in the churchyard.

NORMAN COURT   This development of houses is named after the Norman manor house.

OAKFIELDS   John Giddins built a large house called Oakfields in 1875 for himself and his second wife. He was a farmer and builder who had lived beside the river and owned the boathouse and yard. Oakfields was later pulled down and replaced by modern houses and bungalows.

PAYN CLOSE   Payn de Hemingford inherited the manor of Hemingford Grey from his father, Ralf son of Osmund. It is thought that the manor house and church were commenced in his time. Payn owed to his overlord, Aubrey de Vere, the service of a knight in 1166. In return for holding the land he was required to bring arms, armour and a horse for up to 40 days' active service in a year. It is probable that he died shortly after this date.

PEMBROKE CLOSE   This road takes its name from Pembroke Villa which was pulled down to make room for more houses.

POUND ROAD, OLD POUND CLOSE   A pound was usually at the edge of a village. In Hemingford Grey it was at the end of the High Street on the south east side of Pound Road. At enclosure in 1801, this was just beyond the limit of the village, on the present site of the rosebed. Old photographs show it surrounded by a picket fence.

Before enclosure, the strips in the open fields rarely had hedges or fences. If cattle were pastured on waste or fallow land in the arable fields, they were tethered. Inevitably some strayed. Some owners also pastured more animals than their entitlement. When this happened the animals were driven to the village or parish pound and only released on payment of a fine. Profits from Pound Close paid for the services of the pinder, the villager who was nominated to collect stray animals.

PRIORS ROAD In 1291 the church was known as Hemingford Priors, to distinguish it from the church of Hemingford Abbots. At that time it came under the priory of Huntingdon. When a vicarage was set up in the village, a pension of ½ a mark (roughly six shillings and eight pence or 35p) was reserved to the sacrist of Huntingdon. In 1600 the church was transferred from the care of the Priory of Huntingdon to the bishop of Ely.

RAMPLYS The Ramply family were owners of land offered for sale by Messrs Dilley, Son and Read at St Ives on Monday 4th October 1920. The land was pasture and a market garden near the St Ives road whose tenant was Mr William See. Other fields were occupied by Mr Reed and Mr Sale. These were off Marsh Lane and Gore Tree Road but included a residence in the High Street.

ROSENTHAL TERRACE This row of cottages was originally a three storied malting named after Rosenthal House, the home of John Gifford, a nineteenth century brewer and baker. The other malting in Church Street, now called Cleveland Terrace Cottages, was at one stage in the same ownership. It is not known why the house and cottages bear the name Rosenthal.

SADLERS WAY See Dendys

STEPPING STONES The name is derived from stones used to cross the brook and marshy ground and was a favourite playing place for children.

ST JAMES' COURT These houses are built on land once part of the workhouse. Originally a parish was expected to look after its own poor. Overseers were charged to raise revenue from local residents. It was in the interests of the parish to move on paupers who did not belong to the parish and to find the father of any illegitimate baby so that he could be made to pay for the upkeep of the child and mother. In 1834 the Poor Law Amendment Act introduced a new system whereby parishes joined together in a union to provide for the poor. This led to the building of large institutions one of which was on the site of Limes Park, in London Road. At the time, the parish owned houses which were rented to those not in the Union. In 1851 the workhouse yard contained two families, an old lady of 73 on "parish pay", a form of Income Support, and a James Skinner whose wife had died leaving him with a family of five ranging in age from 20 down to 10. Originally there may have been six cottages. In the 1920's three cottages remained. Mrs Winter started a laundry here to give employment to girls in the village. This then became Gordons, the upholsterers and is now St James' Court, a development of town houses.

THE THORPE It is possible that this is one of the earliest inhabited areas of the parish as the name could be Danish in origin. It would seem that the original village was grouped along the High Street on the south and along the Thorpe. Evidence from 1801 suggests that the land on either side of the Thorpe was part of the demesne, the name given to the land occupied by the lord of the manor which his tenants were expected to work in return for being allowed to grow crops in the open fields. The demesne was also called Home Field and parts of it were enclosed before 1801. In 1851 there were ten families living in the Thorpe, most of whom were agricultural labourers with a few people dependent on parish pay. This had reduced to nine households in 1891 with one house uninhabited. Orchard House was the home of the orchard manager. It contained one room with a concrete floor for the storage of fruit. Most of the present houses were built in the twentieth century.

A list of village charities made in 1896 included a Pest House in the Thorpe. Pest houses were isolation places possibly for people on parish pay who were suffering from diseases such as small pox. By 1896 all that remained was the land and a ruined building. This was pulled down and the bricks reused to make a kitchen at the workhouse cottages in the High Street. The land, which probably adjoined the highway, was let for five shillings per annum. Although the tenant was not allowed to put up any buildings he seems to have had a fowlhouse which caused concern to the parish council. As the parish council was also accused by the cherry orchard manager of blocking access to the Thorpe it is possible that this tenant "acquired" too much land. [37]

TURBERVILLE COURT Ralph de Turberville was lord of the manor in the 13th century. His wife Alice was the great granddaughter of Payn de Hemingford who probably built the manor house. For a while the manor was called Hemingford Turberville after him.

VICARAGE FIELDS This was Glebe land which was part of the income of the vicar. He either farmed it himself or leased it out. There is a distinction between rector and vicar. Originally the rector was appointed to a parish and received the tithes of the parishioners. He was responsible for church services, the spiritual welfare of his flock and for maintaining the fabric of the church. But when the rectory of Hemingford Grey and its tithes was made over to the Priory of Huntingdon, a vicar was appointed in his place who received his payment in the form of the small tithes and performed the religious functions of the church. By the time of the Dissolution of the Monasteries in 1588, the rectory was valued at £17 per annum and the vicarage at £10. The rectory was appropriated by lay people for a time until it came into the hands of the Bishop of Ely.

In 1697 John Allen, the vicar, petitioned "the well-disposed gentlemen of the University of Cambridge and elsewhere for assistance to rebuild the vicarage house, which had fallen into a state of ruin during the late rebellious times". Although this statement has traditionally been thought to refer to the rectory house it is more likely that it refers to the vicarage. The patron of the vicarage was at one time Trinity Hall College in Cambridge and these could have been the gentlemen who offered help. The late rebellious times could have been the Civil War.

In 1801 the vicar, Mr J S Banks, lived on the south side of the High Street on the site of Grey Hall, with farmbuildings and cottages further east. He had about 18 acres of enclosed land in the great marsh, shrub and home fields and the town close. This included the area now called Vicarage Fields. In 1843/4 the Parliamentary Gazette recorded that the gross income from the vicarage was £179 per annum and the house and land were rated at £9.16.10d.[38] In 1854 Grey Hall was extensively altered to make a suitable home for the vicar who had a considerable social position. Subsequently the vicarage was moved to a modern thatched house on the corner of Manor Road and Braggs Lane. When the church sold the Glebe to developers it was on condition that a new vicarage was built in Braggs Lane.

VICTORIA TERRACE This is a row of 38 terraced cottages built before 1851 as a suburb for the expanding town of St Ives. Architecturally it is interesting because it is a very long terrace without an expansion joint.

Of its earliest inhabitants the majority were born in the town. Whereas men in the village largely worked on the land, those in the terrace worked in urban industries, like engineering, building and on the river. There were five watermen who would have manned the barges that carried goods between Kings Lynn and Bedford. There were also two boatwrights to construct the barges, a millwright who could have worked at the St Ives mill, in addition to a grocer, cabinet maker, charwoman, laundress and tailor. Number One Victoria Terrace was a pub occupied in 1851 by Isaac Asplan. Possibly his wife ran the pub as he was also

Victoria Terrace under flood c 1940 (Norris Museum HEM.G/27a)

a waterman employing six labourers. Those who lived here were not poor employees but rather people who had bettered themselves and could afford to move to new houses.

By 1891 changes in the local economy are reflected in the trades recorded. There were no longer any watermen as the goods carried had decreased with the success of the railway but two men worked as railway signalmen. Others involved in transport were a carrier, wheelwright, blacksmith, coach painter and coach wheeler, showing that road traffic was still largely dependent on horses. A postman lived in one house and a painter in another. Four now worked on the land. Six of the heads of households had been born in the village and this time five in St Ives. For the rest, they came from neighbouring villages or even Leicestershire, Bedfordshire, Staffordshire or Oxfordshire. Ease of travel ensured that people could now work much further from their place of birth.

Most of the cottages had two-bedrooms, although families could be large. For example, James Stockwell, a gardener, lived with his wife and five children at number 14. The parents and oldest daughter Annie were born in Oxfordshire, their son Horace in Warwickshire, the next two children in a different village in Warwickshire and only eight year old Ernest in Hemingford Grey. The Queens Head, at number 1, was occupied by Stephen MacQuire, a boatwright born in the village with his wife and four children of 11, 8, 2 and 6 months. This was the only family whose members were all born in the village.

There were two waterpumps in the back road where women and children gathered to chat. Brick privies, which can still be seen in some of the gardens, were provided and the contents of the "bucket " were buried in the garden   Later the Council arranged a weekly night soil collection which must have been the same for the rest of the village. There was no mains sewage until after the Second World War.

Anyone who lived in the Terrace in 1947 remembers vividly the terrible floods and the delivery of food from boats to people sheltering upstairs from the water. April 1998 saw a repeat of the devastation that flood water can bring when the terrace homes were flooded for a whole week and rendered uninhabitable for several months.

VINE CLOSE   This is named after Vine Cottage built before 1902 which has now been replaced by modern houses.

THE VINEYARD   This is said to be the site of a vineyard attached to the Manor House. The name was used in deeds in 1940 but not in 1928. It is not known how the name came into use.

WEIR CLOSE AND WEIR ROAD   These roads are named after the weir which used to be beside the pond on the present site of the village sign in Hemingford Road. The weir controlled drainage water from the village which fed into the brook which ran from the centre of the village to Marsh Lane and thence to Lake Brook and the Ouse in Fenstanton. A disc used to warn people of danger at the weir. It was this brook that was crossed by stepping stones. It was not until the village had mains sewerage that the problem of pollution at the weir disappeared. In 1851 James Giddins and his family lived at "Wharehead" cottage. He farmed 85 acres of land with the help of six labourers, two sons and two daughters.

WESTMEARE   This road lies on the western boundary of the parish on the disused line of the ancient mere way which ran from the river in the direction of Hilton. It still runs south of the A14 to a farm called Meerway Farm and was described in 1801 as being "mostly in Hemingford Abbots from the Cambridge Turnpike at Gore Tree."

Sources

1 H Norris "An English Village", 1888, p 29

2 S Oosthiuzen "The Origins of Hemingford Grey" in Records of Huntingdonshire, vol 3, no 1, 1992

3 VCH, "Huntingdonshire", vol ii., 1932, pp 306-312

4 D Hey, "The Oxford Companion to Local and Family History", 1996, passim

5 Norris Museum and Library, St Ives, copy of the bill and decree of Chancery relating to the inclosure of the manor of Hemingford Grey between Newman and others and the Bishop of Ely and others, 8.2.1670

6 PRO, E179/249/2

7 Hunts Post 4.11.1926

8 HRO, Enclosure Award of Hemingford Abbots and Grey, 1801

9 VCH, Huntingdonshire, vol ii, p 324

10 HRO, will of Mary Bragg, 19.8.1718

11 Norris Museum, decree of Chancery relating to inclosure of Hemingford Grey

12 Norris Museum, undated correspondence from Miss Herbert per E L Watts Esq

13 M Rimmer, "Springboard to Settlement - Developments in the 1860's in the North Kennedy Pastoral District"

14 HRO, 1942/2 Deeds 1702 to 1838

15 HRO, Manorial Court Records of St Ives, 12.10.1704

16 Ken Ballard, "Old Industries of St Ives", 1995. pp 6-14

17 R M Blackley, "The Beautiful Misses Gunnings" in the Connoisseur, 1905

18 J Richardson, "The Local Historian", 1974

19 M P Carter, "An Urban Society and Its Hinterland: St Ives in the 17th and early 18th centuries", PhD thesis, Department of English Local History, University of Leicester, 1988

20 M P Wagner "Not an Easy Church", 1982, pp 35/6

21 Ken Ballard, "Old Industries of St Ives"

22 Albert Goodman, "Potto Brown; the Village Philanthropist" 1878

23 Hatfield's "Gazetteer and Directory of the County of Huntingdonshire" 1854 p 700

24 Ken Ballard, "Old Industries of St Ives"

25 Calendar Committee for Compounding, pp 928-29

26 R Burn-Murdoch "Robert Langley in the Snow" in Records of Huntingdonshire, vol 2, no 10, 1991, pp 2-5

27 Norris Museum, E Pettis "A Plan of St Ives Parish" 1728, mss

28 Hunts Post 23.5.1904

29 Cal Pat 1321-4, p 14

30 Hunts Post, 12.7.1928

31 L M Boston "Memory in a House" 1973

32 D Summers, "The Great Ouse, The History of a River Navigation", 1973

33 T S Willan "Navigation of the Great Ouse between St Ives and Bedford in the seventeenth century", <u>Publications of the Bedfordshire Historical Record Society</u>, XXIX, 1946:

34 Norris Museum, Hunts Post 1/8/03; 8/8/07; 5/9/07; 7/8/1924; Morning Post 3/12/1929

35 ibid, undated correspondence between Mr E L Watts and Mr I Ladds

36 PR0, SP 16/189/94 1630

37 Parish Council Minutes 1898-1899

38 Cam.c.50031 6 4642.85